This book belongs to:

_____

Acknowledgements

To my children Abby, Mahonri, and Moroni, thank you for teaching me what true love is. Abby and Mahonri, your patience, empathy, and the care you give to your little brother Moroni have deeply touched my soul. To Moroni, thank you for being an angel in our lives.

To my husband Jorge, thank you for always giving me wings to fly, for your unconditional love. I love you.

You can find this book in its Spanish version titled:
'Mi hermano no habla, pero su corazón sí'.

Written and illustrated
by Gabby Cornelio

Hi, I am Maho, and I am seven. I love to play with my family, and every day is a mission because our home is blessed with a very special boy. He is my brother, and he is different from the others. He doesn't use words to talk, but he brings us together with a love that grows more and more.

His name is Momo, he is my brother who can't talk, I often wonder why he doesn't speak. I ask my mom, again and again, sometimes it's difficult to understand, but when Momo smiles so wide, I know everything is going to be ok.

We're having fun with magnets side by side, inventing and creating together. We both enjoy a special time...

My mom says Momo gets frustrated because he can't talk, and that's why he cries and explodes.

I see the magic when Mom appears because, with a hug full of love, Momo's smiles reappear.

We are sitting on the couch when Momo touches my hand. He points up and down, making funny sounds. I still don't understand what he is trying to say.

Momo pulls my hand and takes me to the fridge. We feel the cool air and smell the great smells. Momo points to what he wants and smiles.

I found what Momo needed.
What a special time!
I feel like a champion, with
joy I can't hide.
Helping him makes me feel
like a winner,
The hero of our snack-time
dinner.

At night, it's easier to know what he wants. He raises his hands and signs "Milk." This is so clear; we can finally go to bed and dream.

Mom says learning to sign is so cool. With sign language, you don't need to use words; instead, we use our hands to understand each other more.

My birthday is coming in February. Honestly, I don't want money, toys, or gifts to buy.

My deepest wish, pure and true: It's to talk with my brother, just us two, laughing and chatting the whole day through.

Even if my brother doesn't talk, I know just what he wants to say with

loud noises,

oh
grr—

signs, and

pictures; I decode it day by day.

We don't need words to chat or share;

our hugs,

kisses, and

looks show how much we care.

Though his voice might not be clear, his heart speaks to me.

Every sweet gesture and touch shows that Momo loves me very much.

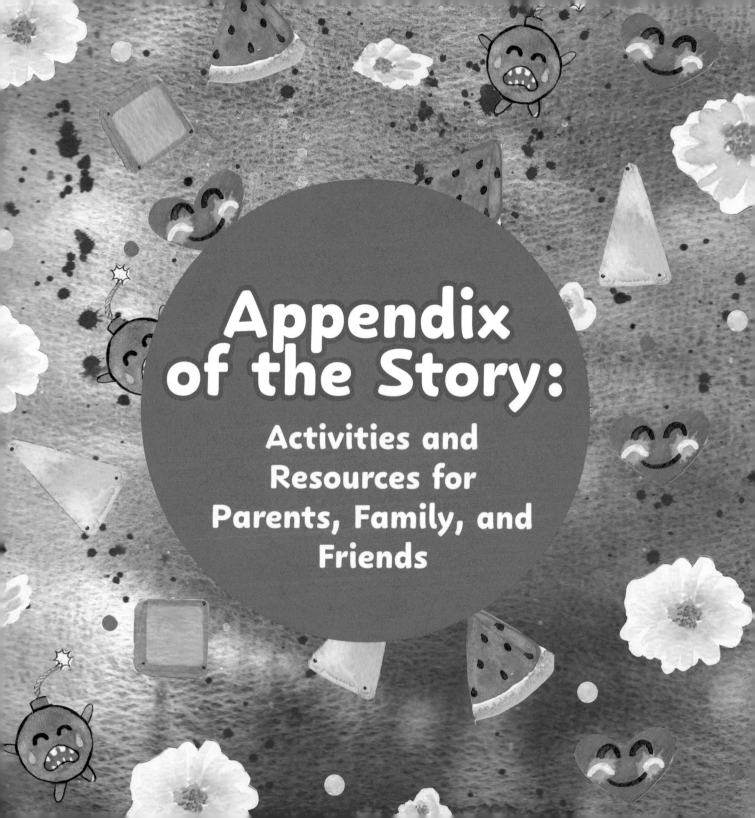

Appendix of the Story:

Activities and Resources for Parents, Family, and Friends

Appendix of the Story: Activities and Resources

Activities for Parents:

You may have come across this story because you are experiencing a similar situation or know someone whose child doesn't speak. This resource has been designed with you and your family in mind. While we don't have all the answers, we share ideas based on our experiences as a mother and a neurodevelopment specialist, with the goal of improving communication and alleviating any frustration that may arise.

How to Foster Communication and Language Skills in Your Child:

1. Look for moments of visual interaction: If your child still doesn't speak, remember that they are listening to you. Modulate your tone of voice and speak clearly, even if they only respond with sounds. This interaction is important for their development.
2. Talk about emotions: Express how you feel so your child can learn to identify and normalize emotions, which promotes empathy and emotional expression.
3. Provide sound experiences: Use musical instruments, mimic sounds, and recognize everyday noises. This not only helps with language development but also with emotional and behavioral self-regulation.
4. Help them identify their sounds: Reflect what you think your child is feeling with phrases like "It seems like you're feeling frustrated" or "It seems like you're enjoying this," even if they don't respond immediately.
5. Use facial expressions and different tones of voice: Practice in front of a mirror if necessary. Your child learns by watching you, and the consistency between what you say and how you say it facilitates their communication.
6. Encourage proper feeding habits: Chewing and biting help develop the muscle tone necessary for speech. Limit the use of pacifiers and encourage breastfeeding to support orofacial development.
7. Don't guess what your child wants: From 9 months of age, model how to ask for things so that your child learns to use words like "water" or "milk."
8. Correct positively: When your child communicates incorrectly, paraphrase what they meant and encourage them to try again. Language develops through trial and error.

What Should I Do If My Child Has a Genetic or Biological Condition That Impedes Speech?

It's important to fully understand the characteristics of their condition and its prognosis. This will allow you to make informed decisions regarding their care, communication, and development.

It is recommended to conduct a comprehensive neurodevelopmental evaluation to identify which areas are affected. Remember that speech is not the only form of communication. There are other methods you can teach your child to communicate effectively. Here are some examples:

1. Sign Language: This is a visual and gestural language that you can teach your child with simple words like "give," "want," "hungry," or "sleep," as well as emotion-related words like "happy" or "sad."
2. Pictograms: These are graphic symbols that represent words or actions. They can be used at home to establish routines or communicate basic needs. You can also use them to identify areas of the house or warn of danger in certain spaces.
3. Communication Boards: These are personalized tools that allow children to communicate using pictures, pictograms, or words. You can create a physical board or use technology, such as a tablet, to help your child express their needs and emotions.

These resources will not only facilitate your child's communication but also give them an effective way to interact with the world around them, reducing their frustration and promoting their emotional and social development.

Activities for Family and Friends:

How Do I Encourage My Child to Communicate with a Child Who Has Speech Difficulties?

Explain that everyone is different, and that's okay because it makes us unique and special. There are many forms of communication, like speaking, using sign language, writing, drawing, or expressing oneself through music.

Help them understand this through social stories, for example:
- The squirrel from Ice Age never spoke, but it made us laugh with its expressions of hunger and its need for the acorn.
- R2-D2 from Star Wars only made sounds, yet everyone still understood what it wanted.

Practice games that develop empathy:
- Express feelings or phrases with signs and let others guess what you want to say.
- Introduce yourself or express emotions using sounds or drawings without using words.

This resource has been developed with the valuable guidance of Nora Elicema Velázquez Félix, a Master in Neurological Rehabilitation, who has shared her expertise to support the development of children with speech difficulties.

Appendix of the Story: Letter from the Author

Hello, I'm Gabby, Maho and Momo's mom.

I want to thank you for choosing this book, which is our story. In it, I share what my children experience every day with their little brother Momo. While the challenges can sometimes be frustrating and difficult, they are also beautiful and deeply rewarding, as they bring us closer as a family and help us develop more empathy towards others. My son Momo's progress has been amazing, and much of it is due to our work as parents: knowing how to stimulate him, finding the right resources for his development, and applying what we've learned day by day.

I want to congratulate you on the work you're doing and encourage you to keep seeking the tools necessary for your child's progress. There are many resources available that can help. One of them is **early child intervention** (ECI), which involves providing care to children during the early stages of life to foster the optimal development of their physical, cognitive, and emotional abilities through structured programs that cover all aspects of human development.

Another important tool is orofacial **myofunctional therapy** (OMT), a treatment that combines physiotherapy and breathing exercises to address issues related to speech, chewing, breathing, and swallowing. This therapy is essential for children who face difficulties with orofacial muscles, which are crucial for these basic functions.

If your child is not speaking yet, I encourage you to explore these resources and seek help from professionals in these areas, as they can make a huge difference in their development.

Remember, the journey of parenting is a wonderful one, with highs and lows, and the key is to have a lot of patience, empathy, and love. Don't give up. You're doing an amazing job!

With love,
Gabby Cornelio

46388469R00015